TAABIIR

INTERPRETATION OF YOUR DEEPEST THOUGHTS

SONALI DANIA

Copyright © Sonali Dania
All Rights Reserved.

This book has been published with all efforts taken to make the material error-free after the consent of the author. However, the author and the publisher do not assume and hereby disclaim any liability to any party for any loss, damage, or disruption caused by errors or omissions, whether such errors or omissions result from negligence, accident, or any other cause.

While every effort has been made to avoid any mistake or omission, this publication is being sold on the condition and understanding that neither the author nor the publishers or printers would be liable in any manner to any person by reason of any mistake or omission in this publication or for any action taken or omitted to be taken or advice rendered or accepted on the basis of this work. For any defect in printing or binding the publishers will be liable only to replace the defective copy by another copy of this work then available.

To all the loving souls,

mortals and immortals.

The ones who believe in me,

with patience and glee.

Contents

Preface

All humans are blessed with complex feelings. To understand those and melt them down to words is the motive of this compilation. This book carries all the emotions of love, hatred, envy, happiness and sorrow. The soliloquy or the self talk presented in the form of poems will make you submerge into your own brain and feel the emotions converting into verses as you read along the lines.

"Taabiir" is an urdu word which means, interpretation. Interpretation of your deepest thoughts and arrange the words together to form the poem thereby, being your messenger. If the lines make you feel the swarming emotions, my purpose is successful.

Happy Reading!

Make a wish, to abolish all fears.
From your lips, to God's ears.

1. Believe

Rumi said, "The wound is the place where light enters you"
So do not in any case, ever feel the blue.
Be strong and stern, just like a stone
Affirmations arising from your bone.
Abide by the words of the holy saints,
Seek the sojourn where the soul acquaints.
Your belief, your credence is a message so plain,
to the almighty, and plead to free you from the pain.
Your true obedience, and mind in awe,
will lead you to a stage with sufferings no more.
Just takea moment to remember your pious lord,
That is the one thing, your love and faith can afford.

2. A bouquet

Wilted sunflowers and lilies in my hand,
time passing by, betwixt fingers like sand
The brain is numb and the heart has so much to speak
my mouth close shut, and the hollow soul shriek
Forgive me for all my mistakes that you see
I assure, from all your complaints, I shall one day set you free
The might just not be today for you to know
FYI, I am just letting the paralysis in my head grow
I will stay where I am right now
waiting with sunken eyes and loosened brow
with dead sunflower and lilies in my hand
As i see myself drowning in the dry sand

3. Winter eve

Cotton falling from the glittery sky,
chilly breeze flowing by
Sitting all wrapped, all plans obdurate
Just to procastinate with some hot chocolate
Oh my wonderful month so cold,
what love and beauty you behold.
For i wish to live forever in this igloo
with white grass and skies deep blue.
As the warmest memories evolve in winter eve,
The loveliest moments that you would never wish to leave.

4. Little things

Can we share a cup of tea,
Betwixt spring breeze and evenings, carefree
to talk about how the day went by,
and share some laughs as I complaint about my boss so sly.
Can we share a bag of chips,
as we recall the memories through our video clips
hidden in your folder, meant only for thy eyes,
reminiscence of those tipsy highs.
Can we share a sheet tonight,
in those chilly hills with stars so bright
and we can touch each others' heart and soul
to let our breaths do the conversation whole
Can we share this love for life
walking down the aisle, as your wife.
To share that cup of tea, every season,
and become a part of each other's crucial discussion.

5. The regained love

I saw him, and I watched him go through
The city lights and sky deep blue.
Subliming into the dust of distance
leaving me alone, with my mere existence.
It's not a story of separation,
that your eyes just see
It's that growing anticipation
that sets my soul so free
to wander alone in the steady streets,
to wander alone in the empty streets
What do I wish today,
from the develi's djinn in play?
To hear your voice everyday,
to feel your touch, when i lay.
I might get cursed to sell my soul,
convert into ashes, in a dark hole,
but why should I fear that sight?
when I solemnly asked this in plight.
For those ashes might sublime in distance
leaving me away from my own existence.
Did I just get what I wanted so bad?
That feeling that I never had

of you stopping by forever
till the last mile, the last endeavour.
I am glad that I won't see you going through
leaving me alone under the sky, deep blue.
Oh! I am so glad that I can have you only for me
dissolving my senses as I watch, I see
you driving through the city lights.
Not away from me!
but this time, coming closer in glee.

6. Stories

She tells many stories,
but never tells her own.
That's how fonder she has gone for the world,
but darker her soul has grown.
Her eyes deep blue,
full of prodigy.
Her actionsboundless, however
to a stern ideology.
You can tell it from her voice,
the melodies that she utters
sensing all the pain
that her music flutters.
Somebody needs to tell her
a story of her own existence.
To highlight her virtues
and praise her persistence.
The beauty in her heart
overlooked by her inner demon
needs to be banished
by hailing Tamon.
The stories that she tells
but never utters her own

She needs to sideline the cruel world
and embrace self love, so grown.

7. Sweet Poison

The mellow, the bliss.
That mesmerizing kiss
That mixed feeling of your affection and hate
whom do I blame? my actions or my fate?
Fate, maybe, since actions is thy result.
To display agony or utmost exult.
For what now what is dwelling in my mind,
to watch self rot or pretend to be blind.
The mellow, the bliss,
And your pretentious kiss
makes me want you more
Till my lungs go completely sore!
The mellow, the bliss
And the enchanting kiss
sens shivers down the spine
like a poison so divine.

8. Midnight verse

Lightless sights
burns me down into ashes of misery.
I tend to collect the reminiscences of my lost spirit
Repenting over a joyous pyrrhic.
Needless desires
Excruciating liars
provoke me tpo create an undying mystery.
I wish to outgrow the ultimate reality
while I drown into dreams of brutality
Feeling lesser attachments,
challenging my establishments
Unknowingly keeping my blood shivery
with toxic chivalry.
Knowing that I am a fallen angel of hate
Trying to improve my entangled fate.

9. Bright nightmares

Dreaming with a lullaby,
that symphony is echoing.
Moving in the stars so high,
Yet, my mind harrowing.
I tripped in my dreams too
what a disturbing sorcery.
My heart, my mind, my soul, all blue
Toxic tincture oozing through my artery
I woke up dizzy,
Paranoid in a melencholic vibe.
Darned or blessed like an izzy
slipping throughout the the thorny slype.
Living in a nightmare,
is not just one person's story.
The hardships arise,
to beware you of an upcoming glory.
The darkest nights will bring brightest days
to strive you through this agony
will take ardous ways
to reach a kallos dream, and a flowery destiny.

10. Moonchild

The setting sun,
the twinkling stars,
And the enchanting moon
Tells a love story,
of being together, yet so far away.
Of utmost persistence and glory,
and that is how lovers' hearts sway.
The fading hope,
like a wanning crescent over a falling night,
slipping down, through a steep slope,
to feed the sleepless eyes, starving for daylight.
But when again the moon rises up the horizon,
like a wolf grows with beautiful wizen.
Realising that I am in love with all their faces,
for only him, i shall shower my love and praises.

11. Damsel not in distress

Walking through a rainbow of despair!
To raise a finger? we do not do that here!
Oh! So you want a tiny girl to stick, to your skin,
and pretend to love your nasty grin?
Just a reminder to the lovely princess,
you ain't no damsel in distress...

12. Failed adoration

DO I deserve this hatred forever?
Of being wronged all the time.
Even when I try hard to sublime
Do I deserve this rejection forever?
Even if I am truthful in heart
and devote myself into their interests and art.
Do I deserve my words to be neglected forever?
Of speaking out loud and clear
and when I cry my soul out sans any fear.
Is this hatred a punishment of a past sin
Of which I assumed to have gained a win
Is it enough to love and be loyal, today
and expect the same in return for even a single passing day?
Is it okay to be called out as a swindler,
Or to be disguisted upon for being a kindler?
It is hard for sure to regain the trust,
but not fair to forever treat with disguist!
To love, to adore, or to hate,
Is stated by the almighty, through one's fate.
However, to pick a choice is purely human deed
to digest or puke, what one does feed.
To try and understand a point of view?

Or to blame and accuse in lieu?

13. Home Sweet Home

One seeks utopia in the chaos,
sticking by the platonic ethos.
Realise the real paradise is hither,
whilst thy childhood and garden grows,
the cruel world will only smother,
but home is where love bestows.
Aimlessly moved through the empty streets,
and fairs that I wander,
Is for a glimpse of sanity and happiness
yet intoxicated I squander.
To that one holy place, I beg to be at, my lord!
Is that breeze that flows at my home, which no land can offer
and afford!

14. The Doon valley

Walking under weeping skies,
citylights glowing like flocked fireflies.
What is it about this city of doon!
Like spring blooming in the month of June..
Sipping wine with some blue cheese
amidst the green hills and forest breeze.
The city where people love and grow
into high spirits, but feet grounded low!
Oh my dearest home so sweet,
full of delight and perfect treat.
To the people who reside in the paradise!
A life that every person might fantasize

15. Melancholy in my rhymes

They tell me, I write so sad
I question what is so bad
about writing a melancholic verse
when all of us see our lives as a curse.
They tell me I write so negative
I ask, if they really seek the positive
of the gifts that the god bestows
through cool rains and when it snows
They tell me I write so stern
I ask, what is your take when you see the world burn
with hatred and abomination,
instead of love and adoration
They tell me I write stories untrue
I ask if it makes you blue
and realize the reality in which you sway
with sins committed every single day.
They tell me how to write a rosy picture
I ask, to heal with a bitter tincture
of loathe and growing chaos
and your brains corrupted with moss.

They tell me, and only tell me what to write,
to see the silver lining and the brighter side
I ask, if that's what they really always see?
Had it been that ways, you yourself would have lived in glee!

16. Die in love

Just know that I will die for you,
in the most torturous ways
But won't feel a pinch of pain
If i see us, together turning into greys
Just know that I will bless you forever
Even if I am darned to hell
For my sins to hurt you,
deserves banishment in the cursing well
Had it been you and I, till we dwell on earth.
I would travel seven seas to be the one deserved
The sole reason, I wish to be blessed by paradise is
because I know, for you the heaven is reserved.
Had it been us till the end,
the end that directs to the zenith above
I would take a stake across my body to breathe in you
and quietus in your purest love.

17. Lover

When the almighty created this earth to roam
Why have you made a filthy prison your home?
When they told my dearest human has died,
I bashed them with their own words- they lied
Disbelief is what I am dwelling upon,
knocking empty doors, yelling in mourn!
Emotionless, I loiter around in disgrace
To seek a shadowed glimpse of my bloved's face.
My spirit is an open furnace for your flame
Yet you leave it cold, Oh! what a shame
Of being in love yet alone. I beg you to not go
and plead to let the moonlight glow
Your separation is like drought, my lips dries,
The bitter dew, wells up in lover's eyes.

18. Conversational anxiety

I get scared of the dark,
and the ghostly breeze
which makes me weak
shivers down my spine, and bones freeze.
I am scared of the laughter,
which might not be on me.
But pity my pretentious soul,
for mockery is what I only see
I am scared of the falling stars,
the ones everyone preach.
What if I untangle my wishes
and difficulties go beyond reach
I am scared of falling in love
and facing another betrayal,
of attaching my soul again
to the endless trust, that might fail.
I am scared of all that care
that makes me feel deprived
of all my capabilities and potential
that slips away in a stride.
I am scared of being scared
forever and it is true.

As I saw myself drowning
and painting the canvas blue.

19. Society

There is a glitch that I see
Hazy, yet free
Spoke words through my brain
yet you call me a sinner
The one from Gotham.
My response you seek?
I do not care, goddamn!
Apologies, chronologies, methodologies
the wheel keeps turning,
and yet you are stuck to limited psychologies.
Not going to blame you
or accuse you for what you believe
Wish you had a wider vision
or just sane eyes to perceive
the glitches! that i see,
are my haul and your spree!

20. The End

Absorb the sun like it is your last day on earth
Love like it is your last breath to take
You never know when the nightmares appear
In real lives like a deadly plague.
Induldge in the fanciest cuisines
get high on the few moments you pave
For you never know if you could taste that cheese
and sip that poison, your teen heart does crave.
Shout and laugh, cry and weep,
Say it out loud to the whole damn world.
Fearless enough to talk about everything,
and yet preciousd forever to your people, like pearled!

9 7 9 8 8 8 8 1 5 3 5 3 6